# WHAT IF I GET A CONCUSSION?

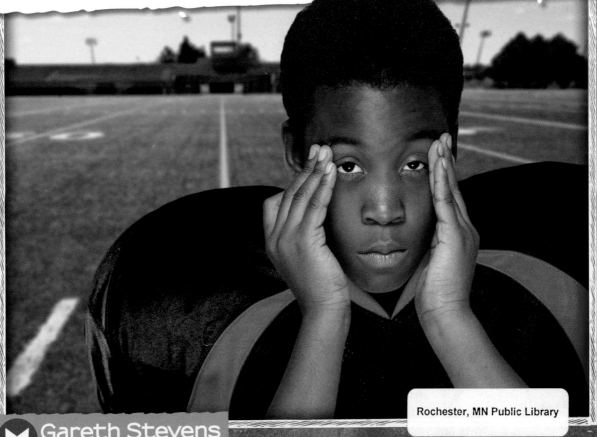

Gareth Stevens
PUBLISHING

BY RYAN NAGELHOUT

Please visit our website, www.garethstevens.com. For a free color catalog of all our high-quality books, call toll free 1-800-542-2595 or fax 1-877-542-2596.

Cataloging-in-Publication Data

Names: Nagelhout, Ryan.
Title: What if I get a concussion? / Ryan Nagelhout.
Description: New York : Gareth Stevens Publishing, 2017. | Series: Benched: dealing with sports injuries | Includes index.
Identifiers: ISBN 9781482448948 (pbk.) | ISBN 9781482448887 (library bound) | ISBN 9781482448412 (6 pack)
Subjects: LCSH: Brain–Concussion–Juvenile literature. | Head–Wounds and injuries–Juvenile literature. | Sports injuries–Juvenile literature.
Classification: LCC RC394.C7 N34 2017 | DDC 617.4'81044–dc23

First Edition

Published in 2017 by
**Gareth Stevens Publishing**
111 East 14th Street, Suite 349
New York, NY 10003

Designer: Katelyn E. Reynolds
Editor: Ryan Nagelhout

Photo credits: Cover, p. 1 (background photo) Benoit Daoust/Shutterstock.com; cover, p. 1 (boy) Tom Le Goff/Valueline/Thinkstock; cover, p. 1 (uniform) Vali Pakalo/Shutterstock.com; cover, pp. 1–24 (background texture) mexrix/Shutterstock.com; cover, pp. 1–24 (chalk elements) Aleks Melnik/Shutterstock.com; p. 5 Sadeugra/Getty Images; p. 7 Hein Nouwens/Shutterstock.com; p. 9 Amy Myers/Shutterstock.com; p. 11 Laszlo66/Shutterstock.com; p. 13 Yavuz Arslan/ullstein bild via Getty Images; p. 15 BSIP/UIG viaGetty Images; p. 17 Lopolo/Shutterstock.com; p. 19 James A Boardman/Shutterstock.com; p. 21 Harry How/Getty Images.

Printed in the United States of America

CPSIA compliance information: Batch #CS16GS : For further information contact Gareth Stevens, New York, New York at 1-800-542-2595.

# CONTENTS

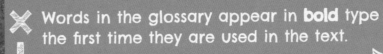
Words in the glossary appear in **bold** type the first time they are used in the text.

# THE UNSEEN INJURY

In sports, **injuries** are often part of the game. Cuts, **bruises**, and even broken bones can force you to the bench to heal up. But some injuries are harder to spot than others. It's easy to see a scraped knee, but how can you tell if you've bruised your brain?

Every day we learn more about brain injuries such as concussions. They're a big problem in all sports. Let's learn how concussions happen and what to do if you suffer a head injury.

# ✕ THE GAME PLAN

**1.** No two injuries are alike. Concussions are tricky to spot, but following some basic rules about concussions can keep you healthy and get you back in the game safely.

Concussions are serious injuries that must be handled carefully. You have to take care of your body, especially your brain!

# COLLISIONS
# CAUSE COLLISIONS

Sports are full of **collisions**, and these big hits can cause concussions. A concussion occurs when the brain bounces off or twists inside the bones of the head, called the skull. The human brain is made of matter kind of like gelatin. This matter is surrounded by a clear, colorless liquid, or fluid.

When the head takes a big hit, the brain can move through the fluid and bump into the skull. This collision can **stretch** the brain and cause harm to its **cells**, even creating **chemical** changes in the brain.

# ✗ THE GAME PLAN

1. Concussions can happen to anyone. It doesn't matter how old they are, how good they are at sports, whether they're a boy or a girl, or even if they wear the right safety **equipment**, including helmets and pads.

fluid

brain

skull

The fluid around the brain keeps it safe from minor bumps and everyday movement, but big hits push the brain through the fluid and into the skull, causing concussions.

# THE CONTACT SPORTS

According to doctors, the most commonly played sports with the highest concussion rates are football, ice hockey, lacrosse, and girls' soccer. But concussions can happen in any sport where the head can hit hard objects or the ground.

Some sports like football or hockey use safety equipment that protects, or keeps safe, a player's head, but very little padding is worn in sports like soccer. A head-to-head hit or a bump on another player's knee might cause a concussion in a low-contact sport.

## ✗ THE GAME PLAN

Head injuries are serious and need careful medical attention. Don't be afraid to ask a coach or parent for help if you're not feeling right. Make sure to keep your safety in mind at all times.

8

# RISKY CONTACT SPORTS

Here's how doctors group different sports and their risk of concussion:

✗ **Highest-risk sports:**
   boxing
   mixed martial arts (MMA)
   martial arts

**Mid-risk sports:** ✗
   basketball
   boys' soccer
   water polo

**High-risk sports:** ✗
   football
   ice hockey
   rugby
   wrestling
   boys' lacrosse
   girls' soccer

✗ **Low-risk sports:**
   baseball
   swimming
   track

Every sport has a certain level of risk for concussion.
Even a fall or bump on the track can cause a concussion.

# SYMPTOMS

So how do you know if you have a concussion? Head injuries like concussions have many different symptoms, or signs of injury. People who suffer a concussion often have more than one of these symptoms, but every concussion is different. Some people get dizzy and have trouble paying attention. Others pass out or even throw up.

Anyone who takes a big hit to the head should be taken out of the game to check for concussion symptoms. A doctor, coach, or some other adult can follow their own concussion training to check if you're okay.

# CONCUSSION SYMPTOMS

People who have a concussion often feel one or more of these symptoms:

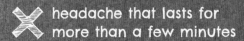 throwing up or feeling like throwing up

 trouble speaking, or saying things that don't make sense

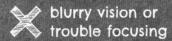 headache that lasts for more than a few minutes

hard time thinking or making decisions

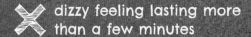 blurry vision or trouble focusing

trouble with balance, catching a ball, or walking straight

dizzy feeling lasting more than a few minutes

You might be just fine after a bump on the field, but if you feel anything, you need to tell someone!

## ✗ THE GAME PLAN

It's usually okay to sleep after a concussion. Also, most people who get a concussion don't pass out. If you do pass out after a hit, however, you need to see a doctor right away.

# GETTING SERIOUS

Some concussions are more **serious** than others. Every head injury should be treated as a serious head injury until a doctor says otherwise. If you think something is wrong, tell a coach or parent you don't feel right.

If you do throw up more than once or have trouble remembering things after a big hit, you could have a serious concussion. Make sure you stop playing right away and ask an adult to take you to a doctor or the hospital.

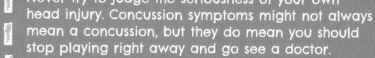

## ✗ THE GAME PLAN

Never try to judge the seriousness of your own head injury. Concussion symptoms might not always mean a concussion, but they do mean you should stop playing right away and go see a doctor.

Concussions are different for everyone. One person may have many different symptoms. Others may only have one or two.

# SERIOUS CONCUSSION SYMPTOMS

If you have these symptoms after a hit to the head, have someone call 911 or visit a doctor right away:

 memory loss

 confused, restless, sleepy, or angry behavior

 throwing up more than once

 headache that gets worse or won't go away

 passing out or getting knocked out

 **seizure**

 had a concussion before

 slurred speech

# GETTING CHECKED OUT

Going to a hospital or doctor's office can seem scary, but it's necessary after a concussion. A doctor will ask you what happened and how you're feeling. Doctors may also test your memory and ability to pay close attention, two things often affected by concussions.

Hospitals usually take scans, or pictures, of your brain to check for injury after a concussion. A CT or CAT scan or an MRI lets doctors see inside your skull! These scans check for any signs of problems with your brain.

# ✕ THE GAME PLAN

1. Doctors also check the rest of your **nervous system** by testing your balance and **coordination**. Some schools have athletes take tests, called baseline tests, before they start playing to see if any big changes happen after a big hit.

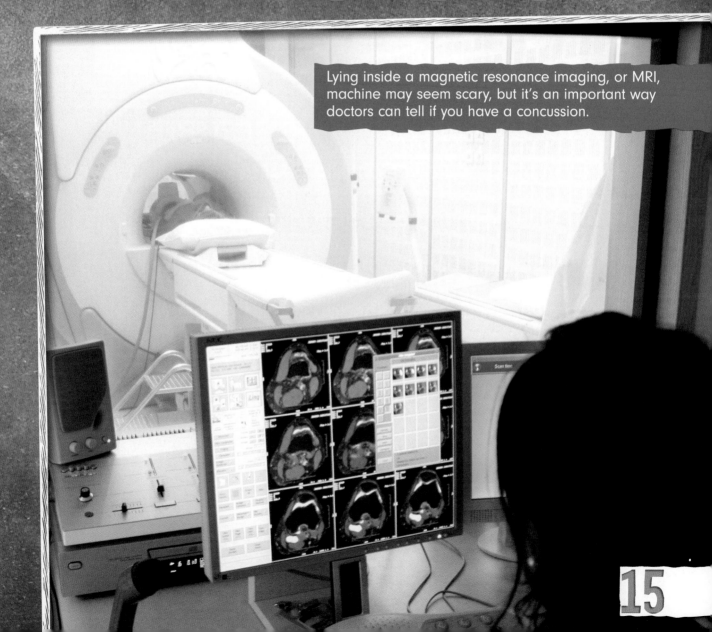

Lying inside a magnetic resonance imaging, or MRI, machine may seem scary, but it's an important way doctors can tell if you have a concussion.

# ON THE BENCH

If you have a concussion, you can't play sports until your brain has been given time to heal. A concussion is just like any other injury: It needs time to get better.

Sitting on the bench is no fun, but it's important not to come back from a concussion too soon. Doctors will tell you exactly what to do during recovery, but you usually can't exercise and need lots of sleep. Make sure you listen to your doctor's orders and tell someone if your head starts to hurt again.

# THE GAME PLAN

1. Sometimes it takes days for concussion symptoms to show up after an injury. Always check for symptoms in the days after a big hit, especially if you don't go see a doctor right away.

Some concussions can keep you out of school, too. Even trying to do homework can give some people headaches when recovering from a concussion.

# BACK IN THE GAME

Remember that only a doctor can tell you when you're ready to play sports again. Your coach might want you back on the field, but you need to be fully healed, or your concussion could get worse. Studies show that the effects of a first concussion can last 6 months to a year.

It also takes kids much longer to recover from a second or third concussion, especially if the concussions happen close together. Always be careful, and protect your head when playing sports!

Second-impact **syndrome** is something that can happen if you play too soon after a concussion. It doesn't happen very often, but another big hit can cause brain damage or even death!

Playing smart is the best way to stay safe on the field or ice. Don't try to hurt others, and make sure to protect your head.

# SID'S STRUGGLE

Hockey superstar Sidney Crosby knows what it's like to come back from a serious concussion. Crosby missed more than 11 months after two hits to the head during the 2011 season. Even after all that time off, Crosby had to be careful in his comeback.

"Concussions are still kind of a mysterious thing," Crosby said. "We do know a lot more now, but there are still things that we can learn." The most important thing is to be careful and tell someone when your head isn't feeling right.

## ✖THE GAME PLAN

Crosby himself noted that concussions aren't like other injuries. The only way to get better after a hit to the head is giving yourself time to get better, and everyone experiences them differently. No two concussions are alike.

# FROM CONCUSSION TO COMEBACK

**January 1, 2011**
Crosby hit by David Steckel
during Winter Classic

**January 5**
Crosby hit by Victor Hedman;
flies to Pittsburgh
for tests the next day

**January 7**
Penguins announce
Crosby has a concussion

**April 29**
Crosby admits
to setback
during recovery

**March 14**
Skates for first
time since injury

**January 28**
Crosby
cleared for
"light workouts"

**January 12**
Crosby ruled
out **indefinitely**

**October 13**
Cleared for
contact
in practice

**December 12**
Crosby out
indefinitely after
concussion-like symptoms

**November 21**
Crosby plays
in first game
since January 5

**January 13, 2012**
Crosby practices again
more than 1 year after
first concussion

# GLOSSARY

**bruise:** an injury that breaks blood vessels beneath the skin, but does not break the skin

**cell:** the smallest basic part of a living thing

**chemical:** having to do with the makeup, structure, and properties of matter

**collision:** an instance of coming together with great force

**coordination:** the ability of different body parts and systems to work well together

**equipment:** the gear used to play sports and protect those playing sports

**indefinitely:** until further notice

**injury:** hurt or loss to the body

**nervous system:** the body system made up of the brain and nerves that moves information throughout the body

**seizure:** a sudden movement of the body showing signs of unusual brain activity

**serious:** important or in need of attention

**stretch:** to move something beyond its usual limits

**syndrome:** a group of things that happen together and show something is wrong with the body

# FOR MORE INFORMATION

## BOOKS

Goldsmith, Connie. *Traumatic Brain Injury: From Concussion to Coma.* Minneapolis, MN: Twenty-First Century Books, 2014.

Hudson, Maryann. *Concussions in Sports.* Minneapolis, MN: ABDO Publishing, 2014.

McClafferty, Carla Killough. *Fourth Down and Inches: Concussions and Football's Make-or-Break Moment.* Minneapolis, MN: Carolrhoda Books, 2013.

## WEBSITES

**Concussions**
*kidshealth.org/parent/general/aches/concussions.html*
Find out more about concussion symptoms and how to deal with head injuries.

**Concussions: What to Do**
*kidshealth.org/teen/safety/first_aid/concussions.html*
This site helps you understand what steps to take if you think you have a concussion.

**What Is a Concussion?**
*cdc.gov/headsup/basics/concussion_whatis.html*
Learn more about what concussions are and how they occur at the official Centers for Disease Control and Prevention website.

# INDEX